Lessons of Little Sweet Woman

Gloria Rueden

To order additional copies of this book, contact:
Xlibris
844-714-8691
www.Xlibris.com
Orders@Xlibris.com

ISBN: Softcover   978-1-6641-6832-9
        EBook   978-1-6641-6831-2

Print information available on the last page

Rev. date: 04/08/2021

Lessons of Little Sweet Woman

Hi! I'm little sweet woman. I'm five. It's the first day with my grandmothers and grandfathers on my mother's and father's side of the family. I have an older brother and older sister and one little brother. My little brother came with us too. His name is great spirit walker eagle warrior. My little brother and I are going to learn all our grandfather's and grandmother's knowledge about the old ways. It's going to be hard work! We had to get up really really really early! It was a long drive from the city.

We get there as the sun is coming up. It's a small house and as you walk in there are plants hanging every ware.

The smells are different it's hard to describe. As we walk to the kitchen each smell changes a little. Some of them make me sneeze and sneeze and sneeze.

Grandmother say it's okay. It's just my bodies way of saying it don't like that one. Our grandmother's sit us down and give us a big breakfast. Grandfather's say we better eat up. We are going to have a long day. Our brains need food to learn. Grandfather's and grandmother's say there goodies to mother and father as we eat. Both grandfather's are drinking coffee. Both grandmother's are drinking tea.

When we are done eating one grandmother takes our plates and the others grandmother lays the plates for grandfather's. Grandfather's eat while we are washing up. When grandfather's are done one grandmother takes their plants and the other lays new ones out. Then grandmother's eat. As grandfather's smile and watch use swerm. Little brother looks just as confused as me. Grandmother's ask why I'm so quiet. I ask grandmother's why do we eat like that. It's because children are the future, mothers and fathers are the present and grandfathers and grandmothers are what has happened. Not the past but the ones to teach the past to the future. There's wisdom in that. I ask why is older brother and sister not here? Grandmother's says everyone has their place in the family. Father has your older brother to teach about the ways of the world. Mother has your older sister. Grandfathers have your little brother. We have you. That way you help each other as you grow up. Why do you say grandfathers and grandmothers, and father and mother? Why not just say mommy and daddy and grandpa & grandma? It's out of respect. A long time ago, all the grandfathers and fathers was grandfather and father to all the children. All the grandmothers and mothers was grandmother and mother to all the children of the whole tribe. So every one called mothers and fathers, and grandfathers and grandmothers out of respect from the other families in the village. That's right.

When grandmother was finished they got me a step tool and we did the dishes together. One grandmother would wash. I would rinse, brother would dry, and the other grandmother would put away the dishes. Why do we do dishes this way? So, we can go together. So, we don't leave scares on the earth as bad.

Then we go out with baskets in hand. Grandfather's go with brother on the lawn working on something. As we walk through the woods, we are picking up twigs that have fallen off the trees in the winter and taking White Burch bark off the fallen trees. The bark will be for medicine and the twigs will be to mark ware other herbs, flowers, and food pants are. We then walk the field finding berries, potatoes, and flowers for medicine.

Grandmother stand up and looks at the sun. Why did you look at the sun grandmother? It's telling me the time you see when the sun is over head and you shadow is small it's around noon. We heard back and walk in the house with grandfather's and brother. Grandfathers asked what I learned to day. Grandmothers ask brother what he learned to day.

The house is so full of talking and clinking of pots, I didn't think anyone would like so much noise. It's okay because grandfather's and grandmother's said it reminded them of good time from long ago. Well got to go eat till next time!!!

Printed in the United States
by Baker & Taylor Publisher Services